PRECIPICE POETRY

For the God-lover
who's been on the brink and back!

Wyetha Prevost

PRECIPICE POETRY
For the God-lover who's been
on the brink and back!

Copyright © 2021 Wyetha Prevost
Cover Design C. Marcel Wiggins

Published by MIGMIR Company USA, LLC
All rights reserved. No part of this publication may be reproduced, distributed or transmitted in any form or by any means, without prior written permission. Unless otherwise identified, scripture quotations are from the King James Version of the Bible.

Dekan Press
an imprint of
MIGMIR Company USA, LLC

www.migmir.us

For Worldwide Distribution
Printed in the U.S.A.

ISBN: 9781952253133
Library of Congress Control Number: 2021932334

TABLE OF CONTENTS

Acknowledgments. 6
Introduction 10
Making War 12
Innocence Stolen — Just Like That 15
Counting Sheep 16
Yesterday I Cried 18
I Went Away 20
Cycle 22
Bitter Heart 25
Angel Song 27
Something to Think About 28
But Did You Die? 29
On Waning Vision 30
The Tongue 33
Who Gets Mad at the Dead? 34
Sorry for Myself 36
Chosen 37
Fractured 39
Breaking Point 40
Call to Arms 42
After Thought 43
Run 44
History 45
Groom 46
Hush 47
Dark Room 48

TABLE OF CONTENTS CONT.

No Shoes 50
No Mere Existence 52
House of God 53
Kingdom Warrior 54
Out of the Ashes 55
One Drop 56
Peace Like a River 57
O Captain 58
Potter's Wheel 60
Prayer 61
Proclamation 62
Promise Keeper 63
Proposal 64
Questions and Answers 65
Pslams 107:2 66
Rapture 67
Rebuke 68
Sonlight 69
The Storm 70
3 A.M. 71
Throne Song 72
Why existence? 73
When I Meet You 74
Words from the Broken Place 75
Thoughts of the Blood 77
Winter No More 78

Worried	80
What If?	84
The Threshing Floor	89
The Other Shoe	90
The Cost	96
My Own Rivers	98
In the Shadow of Death	100
Deaf John Letter (A break up)	104
Conversation with a Counterfeit	109
Wedding Day	112
God is a Murderer	113

ACKNOWLEDGMENTS

To the love of my life — confidant and protector, my ride or die: I have dragged you on every single adventure and you never (almost never) complained. It has been 30 years and counting, and I know it is cliché, but I really do love you more now than I ever did. My love is still growing with each passing day. I love you Marvin Thomas Prevost!!! You would have a fundraiser for a trip to the moon if I decided I wanted to go. You believe I can do anything, and that makes me feel like I can. Thank you for being my #1 fan. You are my soulmate. It's me and you babe. "We gonna conquer the world." Infinity with you sounds like the ultimate plan. There is absolutely no one else I would spend my life with. Your love for me is tangible. You give me breath everyday. I was created to be your wife!

To my grown up babies: There are no words to describe the love you created in my life! Thomas, Kyle, and Zoe, thank you for living a portion of this crazy life with me that led to the writing of my first book. Thank you for being a listening ear when I acted as if I was the best poet on the planet. Zoe, thank you for always being excited to tag along to all of the spoken word events, talent shows, and

Arts & Open Mic events. Thank you for being proud of your mom, and thinking I was cool enough to invite your friends to tag along.

"Well, Ann Moore would ya looka here!" I did it! I did it! Your verbal assaults told me to write poetry and demanded that I complete my book. Also, for listening to my ideas and catching a whole attitude when I did not execute them. I love and thank you for it all. Everyone needs a "Dr. Valerie Moore-Burris" to believe in their work.

To Paula McFarland-Jones, the most gorgeous definition of Black Girl Magic to ever exist, you always act as the listening ear for my new poetry, and are genuinely eager to hear it. Thank you, thank you, thank you for your honest critique and for being as excited as I was when God downloaded words into my spirit. You sat "front seat" at every open mic smiling like the sun. We've been legit friends for so long that I cannot remember how we came to be in the first place. I love you girl! My truly best friend, you have been my thick and thin — there to witness so many of the situations that created the smiles, and the tears, and the muse for my penned words.

Aunt Susan Hairston, losing you was the ultimate punch in my gut screaming get it done! Before you left, you said you were gonna be on me until I got it done. I cry knowing you can't read it. Your heart always pushed us to love God and accomplish... Auntie, you would be proud as I have done both! Rest well my Ladybug. See you later.

Lastly, thank You Jesus for the ultimate love You show me. I am grateful I have survived this crazy life. You thought enough of me to give me the gift of word and mind. Your downloads are the ultimate lessons of life. My Savior, I praise You! Thank you Judas for being faithful to your job. Your schemes brought balance to this book.

INTRODUCTION

Poetry — I didn't know that it could be a source of refuge; a path to deliverance. What wonderful gifts our Heavenly Father blesses us with, yet we do not realize their healing qualities. I had no idea it was something others wanted to hear until my daughter, and best friend began telling me how amazing I was. I am a novice, I must admit. Yet, my head has been pumped up by a few family members and a couple poetry open mics.

On a serious note, I wrote Precipice because I have survived some major life hurdles. How many times and ways can you nearly die physically, emotionally, mentally, and spiritually, but then just don't die? No, I didn't die! I wanted to because it seemed easier than life. I even tried to help death along after losing my younger brother to a motorcycle accident. For some reason God did not allow me to do anything more than vomit, lay weakly on the couch and cry. I was so broken and confused that I believed I couldn't even die right. That is when I wrote, "God is a Murderer." God gave me insight and strength to not just exist, but to also live! There is a difference.

The words penned in this book are for you. Read a sad poem when you are sad. You can be in the moment, just don't stay in the moment. Read a poem of victory in celebration of deliverance, even if you are still on the path. Precipice is meant to serve notice that you're not alone in the good, the bad, and the ugly of life. If you are reading it then you've got another chance. Keep pushing, praying, and praising. God is working it all out — all of it! (Yes it's cliche) Fight the good fight. Take my advice, and write it down, that way, you will have a reason to lift your hands and worship when you realize how you've made it over! May this book of poetry create strength and resilience inside of you. Prayers!

Making war

The very hosts and hounds of Hell have encamped
Among the trees.
I hear the whispers and howls at night as they
prepare to devour me.

I wondered what I must have done to bring attention
To the enemy's camp.
My existence seems so trivial and my worship a
Minuscule flickering lamp.

Attack after attack some I narrowly escape.
My very being feels as if it has suffered rape.

Darkness encroaches and I stoke my pit of fire to
Liven up the flames.
The light the heightened flames give off warms the
Bones of past war pains.

On the East horizon and on every other side,
The enemy scouts out territory and my fleshly
Thought is to just escape and hide.

They have become formidable opponents and my very insides begins to moan.

I once again stoke the fire and my spirit begins
                                        to groan.

    Utterings my ears cannot ascertain yet my soul
                                Catches the vibe.
    The master manifests deep inside and I match my
                            Heartbeat with his stride.

The weapons I have at my disposal for the fight are
                            Ancient yes it's true.
The ancient weapons are fortified and with each
                        Victory they've been proved.

My enemy knows it cannot take my camp by day so
                        He is patient 'til loss of light.
But does my enemy also know that the full moon
                    Brings a heightened sense of fight?!??

My salvation is ever nigh and I feel it's presence all
The more near. Is this the ten thousand at my right
            Hand that the Word of God said "don't fear?"

    My heart waxes within me as I call to mind past
Fights and strife. How many are the seasons of war
                    Did I narrowly escape with my life?

I breathe a sigh of heaviness realizing tonight might be the night.
I spied a rebel scout among the trees measuring me up while lurking just out of plain sight.

Is there another fight in this wretched soldier, can I
Once again stomach the wounds of war?
This time will I again obtain victory or watch my very own blood and water pour?

Will I be deemed a coward if I just keep head and
Sword both down?
Is it weakness to mingle among the thoughts that
Accepting a death blow would quickly bring a crown?

After all, I have fought many good fights and have
Managed to keep the faith.
It's obvious in this life I live that pain is something I
Will never escape.

I have been given the gift of endurance and it's one
I'd rather return. I have been in war so long that it's
Only for peace that I yearn.

After much trepidation I reassure myself
That this duty of war is a soldier's
Pledge. At sunrise I shall wait no longer
And I will attack and take my enemies
Down by the sword's edge.

Innocence stolen – just like that

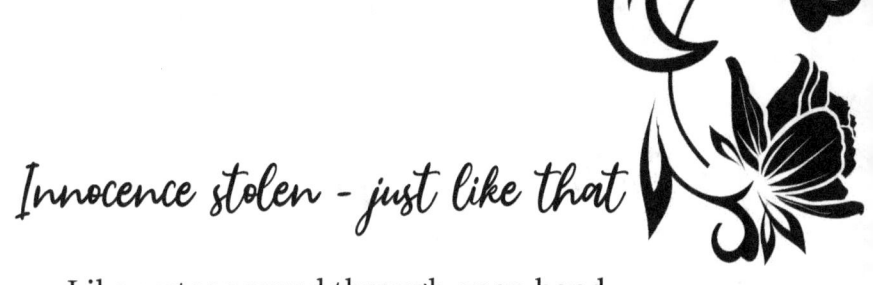

Like water poured through open hand.
Like fingers muddled through soft beach sand.

Like laughter at the point of death.
Like dreams deferred because of theft.

Like a mind diseased from cancer fought.
Like a child abducted, the perp uncaught.

Like witty ideas whispered to a spy.
Like a moment past 'twas time to cry.

Innocence stolen...I lost you... Just like that.

Counting sheep

1 mind racing at the speed of light
2 eyes glaring at the tiny night light
3 voices quarreling in my head
4 fears flooding in with massive dread
5 times I tried to blot it all out
6 times flooded with waves of doubt
7 prayers to numb the pain
8 times a night I am back here again
9 minutes an hour is what I sleep
10 minutes an hour is what I weep
11 days ago I thought to go to Heaven
12 times I reached way back to seven
13 a number not unlucky to me
14 is the count of letting powers be
15 times I feel the demonic haze
16 time on my behalf the angels rage
17 nights the month half gone
18 thoughts of how much can go wrong
19 episodes of watching night turn to day
20 days of wishing sunrise would go away
21 eves of realizing I survived

22 days of plans to revive
23 prayers of begging God to explain
24 of His plans and reason for my pain

25 it happens to be my favorite number
26 days of unprofitable slumber

27 days another month done
28 down and almost back at one
29 nights I vow to pray again
30 nights I ask God if it is because of sin

One day I realize I never counted sheep
But I always pray the Lord my soul to keep

Yesterday I cried

For what I could not control.
For what I could not recreate whole.
For what I could not make new.
For all that was said that wasn't true.

Yesterday I cried.
For what passed away without final farewell.
For disaster I unable to curtail.
For fights with those who made me sad.
For words I wished I'd never had.
For purpose fully unrealized.
For failure of hopes fully prized.

Yesterday I cried.
For life slipped away to soon.
For dreams deflated like a balloon.
For every breath not inhaled deep.
For every tear engrossed in weep.
For every hour slipped away.
For every soul that could not stay.

Yesterday I cried.
Day slipped by and turned to night.
While heavy again my tears I fight.

Tonight as night slips into day.
These frustrated tears will soon pass away.

For tomorrow I refuse to cry.
Maybe I won't sob maybe I'll just sigh.
Lift the heavy of the year so that I may remember a
Yesterday without a tear.

I went away

The air was thick and stale. Stagnation stood shoulder to shoulder with me as I yearned for my solitary space. Stardom struck all around but boredom was my lot.

What would become of me? Me who could only vocalize witness of the breath of God because my chest had not ceased to attend to its mandated motion of up and down responsibilities.

I wasn't tender I was bitter. I wasn't whole I was fractured. I wasn't powerful I was waning. I wasn't healthy I was bleeding. I wasn't living I was existing.

Hall of mirrors were the souls around me finally giving up and giving back to me what I had been parceling out to each of them. Reflections of the ugly, of the hopeless, of the dead undead soul that I was fostering inside myself.

Inside myself, now that is a concept. That is where I

went when I went away. Inside myself... Can't I see that there is exactly where I cannot stay... I went away... inside

myself and I pray that my ticket was not one way.

Exhale, turn, march on, in the direction I came. The exit is near. Can I see it. Wow that looks too far to walk...but if I came this far then I can go that far.

I drifted, I shifted, I morphed, I melted. Wandered, slid, faded and fretted my way right into this sullen desolate place.

I tell myself just keep walking toward the exit and use the strength you have left to leave this stagnant place. Remove yourself from the place you went away.

I tell myself remove yourself back to life, remove yourself back to hope, remove yourself back to HIS presence.

Cycle

With mingling of flesh was I spilled into my mother's womb. The very nature of sin and iniquity's shape swelled my mothers belly. What shall I say except woe unto me!

I, this wretch undone that the snake on his slimy belly should be my undoing? Nay! Not he! For he is but a foe though a formidable one. The lust of the eye, the lust of the flesh, and the pride of life is the wicked trinity.

The veiled powerhouses so willing to glory and relish in the concept of taking me to my grave incomplete of destiny, incomplete of victory, and incomplete of completeness.

Shall I give it to them? Shall I render my soul to the unholy three? After all were they not within me before me was a me? A death sentence before life even began. Listen to the judge, listen to his diagnostic description of his own creation. YOU were

BORN in SIN... YOU were SHAPED in INIQUITY.

As I go along my days, a path of weeks, months, and years progress at the speed of light and suddenly I recognize that the

ignoble three of lust, lust, and pride has stoned my heart, weakened, my flesh, walled in my soul. Still there is a flicker of light within the boundless pit of hell that has come to be known as my life.
A whisper, I think it bids me come and presents a path straight ahead. Though, I cannot see the source beyond the horizon. The stones beneath my feet have turned crimson bright and I am unafraid.

What has taken hold of my stoned heart as I feel it melting within me. My knees buckle though I feel the weights being lifted. Me, a plethora of contradictions: scared to death yet unafraid, heavy, yet light as a feather, at peace, yet feel a war brewing on my behalf, smiling through tears, full of shame yet beaming with new clean hands.

Who has come to save me from the plight of man that has been the plight since man was man? Who has made their own blood recompense to creator that my blood should not be spilled.

Who did not shudder under the sound of gavel and declaration of guilty with final judgment. DEATH He planned this whole thing (I whisper realizing that I was rescued before I was conceived) HE PLANNED THE WHOLE THING!

Creator had no intention of leaving me to my own demise, no intention of leaving me to be consumed by lust, lust, and pride. My eye turned to him, my flesh locked down by spirit, and my pride now bowed to HIM. Born again! The first birth a birth into death, aye but second birth a birth to everlasting life.

Bitter hearts

Drinking poison that you have stirred.
Rehashed conversations never spoken or Heard.

Fiercest arrows aimed at heart.
Wounded pride felt from the start.

Wrestle against flesh and blood no victory Will be Obtained.
The war must be waged in Heaven using Hands Without a stain.

Search yourself and inventory take.
Fake humility leaves fools and destruction In the Wake.

Stop the bleeding of your own emotion.
Flooding in like tumultuous waves upon Life's Ocean.

Hear the breath flowing from your enemy's throat.
Let the memory of love and compassion you once Had be the jolt.

Turn your feet in the opposite way.
No room for bitter and grievous thoughts to stay.

Exhale the harmful touches felt .
Release the bruise from death blows dealt.

Raise your hands up toward the sky.
Let bitterness, frustration, and anger fly.

Angel song

Angels do forever sing.
Holy, Holy is the King.

As they bow around the throne.
To Heaven and the earth be known.

All creation joins in singing.
Until the mountaintops are ringing.

Join ye in the angels' song.
A melodious piping from the throng.

For He who sits is crowned with light.
Aiding all men in each his plight.

Oh, humankind lift voice and sing.
In harmony and joy You bring.

A sweeter sound to the angels' song.
Flesh join them now and sing along.

For angels do forever sing.
Holy, Holy is the King.

Something to think about

Every ending is just the pathway to a new beginning. The sun shines on the day starting somewhere else and makes its global trek to you just as you are closing your eyes on the one you currently occupy.

Frantic mind as pillow meets head... secrets of the day come flooding back with dread... tomorrow I will... tomorrow I won't... drift and dream... ooh dreams, the residence of unspoken hopes and unquenchable fears.

Deeper into the night moment by moment becomes impending day. So much to think about. Hindsight is twenty-twenty, from the end you see it all, the path, the framework, the reason, the victory and defeat. When the sun is shining, the clock obscures view. No why, how, or even when... just process... now process... right now process... so again lay your head on your pillow as the day turns into night turns into day turns into tomorrow, yesterday which is still yet today will become tomorrow in turn making

it today... will once again make today which becomes yesterday... clear... just something to think about.

But did you die?

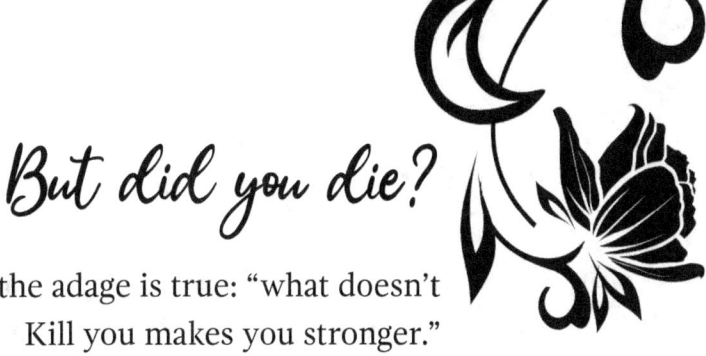

I realize the adage is true: "what doesn't Kill you makes you stronger."

Life has a peculiar way Of pushing us humbly through situations That make us feel as if we are drawing our Last breath.

We decide that not breathing might be Better but still we continue to breathe. Loss makes us count what we lose, taking Inventory of what we no longer have and We rarely dare look at the Substance of what we obtain as greater than what we lost.

Realize that the sum total of our loss Can never compare to what was paid in Exchange for us to Actually have everything.
The death of the ultimate Son on the Unyielding cross is the reason we are not consumed by exhaustive loss.

On waning vision

Riding down highway 77 I stared out of the partially hazed window. With my finger, traced the raindrop path to the bottom. Suddenly, my face matched the window as teardrops raced down and dripped from my chin and tip of my nose. I didn't whimper or sniffle because it was deeper than that. My very soul felt wounded, neglected, and left scarred.

I spoke to Him anyway because that is all I know. "It's been hard" so hard in fact, I can't remember ever having anything go easy in my life. Don't get me wrong Father, I am not so much complaining as I am voicing hurt and confusion. I am flawed in every way, I lack in too many areas, yet my heart is to please you and see your face. Without disrespect can I say that my life feels as if I was destined for your punishment from day one.

There are times when I feel your cares, and times I feel your crushing. It seems that the crushing is much more prevalent and evident.

I can't recall a sweatless victory. For the past 35 years I cant remember having a smile without a storm cloud hanging

over my head. I honestly can't remember when I gained without loss either

preceding or following close on its heels. When people say, "God has never let me down," I don't know what that feels like because I feel as if I am so low to the ground and you see me and step over me. I talk to you, I trust You as my all-knowing Father, I know beyond a shadow of doubt, that You are all powerful and can do all things.

I have followed every instruction given by every prophet. I have prayed on my own, and called on the elders. I have sought out repentance in case I brought this on myself. I have fasted, anointed, quoted your Word to You and to myself, referenced all the miracles I have witnessed you do. I have spoken life when the report was grim. I have sowed multiple seeds (these days every one is a sacrifice).

My faith in what You can do cannot ever be challenged. Yet, I am still in this place. Lord, I have shouted and worshiped reminding myself that it is not what I see now, but will be seen.

Every morning I pop my eyes open telling myself "He did it. He did it. I am healed." Yes, I check while preparing to lose my mind with worship and thanksgiving. This is not the case. I have to resort to thankfulness for just being able to see at all.

My praise is humiliated. People tell me that I lack faith. They must not really know me... 10 years and I still don't need the heart surgery they promised! Ohhh, I have faith! Why are you silent in the matter of my eyes? Why am I suffering without a touch that only my father can give? Why am I alone? What am I missing? Is my life always going to be hard? Is this just the next chapter?

I do not know how to pass this test. I do not know how to get Victory in this trial. I just know I am so lost and confused this time. Nevertheless, I will serve You. Nevertheless, I press forward. Nevertheless, I love You Nevertheless, Nevertheless, Nevertheless.

The tongue

Careful careful what you say your throat an open grave.

The unruly member rules you well, yourself you Cannot save.

Stop your brooding, boasting, bragging
Stop your Raging, gossip, judging.
Send the noise up to the Heavens a joyful tune Meant for the throne.

Can't you see what you say, the power to create.
Can bring a portion of life or death to each advancing day.

Make sure to take care what you say your throat an Open grave.
Or the Creator of hope for a brand new day.

Who gets mad at the dead?

I admit that I was foolish enough to think that if I was there, hovering, feeding cleaning, humming, whispering, and doing anything else that might make you appear as if you are still a healthy part of our world that the death angel might just forget that your name was somewhere on his dreadful list.

Imagine the blow I took, my arrogance shattered when I received the call that I was superficially acting as if would never come. What happens when we ask God for a thing but then remind ourselves aloud that we want His will to be done?

I admit that a bit of underlying schizophrenia erupted. I became double-minded bouncing back and forth between the heartache of finally releasing my sweet one and the joy you would float into as your soul was implanted in a new body, free from the qualms of life.

What can we do to make you stay? I will become

angry with you, then the manipulation of you needing to appease my anger would cause you to not ever try to leave

me. I will pretend that I don't need you. That way, if and when you depart, I could pretend that I wouldn't miss you... pretend we weren't close, and I don't care what you do. How about we do all these amazing things together. That way, you would feel like life was too exciting to depart. You would fight even harder to stay with me. Manipulate your emotions, make you see the foolishness and selfishness in leaving us. What about your mom and dad? How you gonna break up the sisterhood? Let's not even talk about the fact that you are leaving your babies behind to face life and all their amazing milestones without you. How dare you leave us...any of us...all of us. Oh God help me not be upset with her for leaving us, because we all watched her fight like hell to stay here with us all... 'til the end.

Sorry for myself

I cried until I could not see but you bottled every tear I shed. Tears of sorrow for myself and others whose demise has fallen upon my softened heart and drifted before my eyes.

I cried until the ducts were dry and salty was my face. Broken from this burdened life and shaken in this place. Come to me Lord, heal this broken soul and mend the fractured pieces. Deliver me from wretched hands, violence and even leaches.

I cried until my breath is stuttered and my head throbbing with pain, the words of others whisper screaming almost deemed me insane. In all I cried my hope still contained... one thing for certain two things for sure God carries me through all I endure.

I cried until I could not see but you bottled every tear and you are keeping me so after it is all said and done I will rise up and run this race and point my face toward your face.

Chosen

You walked into that broken place.
I stood out in the crowd.

The rattiest one in the bunch.
And you proclaimed aloud.

I'll take that one the dirty one
The one with scar and stain.
I'll take that one the sullen one
With fear, scowl, and disdain.

Come go with me
I heard His voice speak oh so softly now.
What should I do?
Should I stand still or should I quickly bow.

My head hung low in sin and shame
He reached beneath my chin.
Raised up my face now eye to eye
Child, never look down again.

Yet instead toward my face
Always to the sky.
Walk tall my son and dress in grace.
Never more to die.

You will be clean and dressed in white.
The King's offspring you'll now be.
Stand, take My hand, come be My child.
Now you are royalty.

Fractured

Life has fractured most of us...
We believe ourselves whole yet it's clear
We are not because we fall apart at every
Hand.

Broken pieces cavalierly glued together by the
Opinions of others, a need to fit in, desire of things,
Frivolous relationships that only fill a temporary
Void leaving us more empty than when we first
Endeavored.

Most of us drift onto the shores of life on fragments
Of a shipwrecked vessel (us).
We do not know our own hearts,
Minds, or souls and therefore, are a target for the
Arrows of our enemies.

We even paint the bullseye by opening ourselves up
Here's to political correctness, religious heresies,
And disloyal loyalties.

Breaking point

I have begun to feel the pull
Of struggle and heartache both.
The heaviness of daily toil
Disheartens me the most.

Yet, I know so deep within
No shadow of a doubt.
The One I call the Holy One
Is keeping up the count.

When I get to the breaking point
And can withstand no more,
The Writer of my destiny
Shall cast upon the floor.

All the struggle, all the strife
Which has made a vigorous attempt
To snuff out my life.

A standard, a flood
My Protector will raise
For only by His hand
Are my enemies at bay.

With His blessings and His favor
    The Holy One will anoint.
  And move me into victory
      Before the breaking point.

Call to arms

Stand ready for battle
Soldiers of the Cross.
For the time has come
I have burned away the dross.

For the day of all days
You have been prepared
To wage war upon the enemy
If you would dare.

Take sword and take shield
Enter war now go.
Tear asunder here and there
Deal the enemy a deadly blow.

Be fierce with your weapon
The words from the throne.
Take nothing from satan
To his kingdom be known.

To all minions of Hell

To the dark and lowly one.
Your reign has just ended
Your work here is done.

After thought

Favor is poured out on me.
Joy, I can no more contain.
Because You daily bless my soul
My heart utters Your name.

In a city steeped with war.
Refuge I must find.
Mass derision of shattering fear.
Deign enters my mind.

Through this darkened valley of death,
I am aware I must pass through.
But death is but a mere shadow
When I walk close to You.

Run

Run well this race.
Attain the prize.
Keep the faith
Do not despise.

Find peace and solace
In truth and right.
Run the race.
Fight the fight.

Train to endure.
Train to win.
Preparc for victory
Before you begin.

Set the pace.
Blaze new trail.
Set your heart toward Heaven.
You shall not fail.

Run well this race finish on top.

Press on, press on
Do not stop.

History

When they look back and story is told.
How one man came and broke the mold?

Changed certain death into new life.
Removing all our need for strife.

To human kind an architect
The Spirit of God could now connect.
He would be called and forever be
The writer of man's history.

If we would choose a better story told
Than one's created centuries old.
When we carried out our own wicked plan,
And so were separated, God and man.

But….His book of pages infinite
Replaced the ones full of regret.
His wondrous plans deeply hold.
All life's issues in its fold.

To immerse us deep within His Glory
And given to us finally His story.

Groom

One day You'll come to call for me.
And take me as Your own.
Dressed in light 'eh royalty.
Flesh of my flesh now bone of my bone.

Your glory You bring with You.
As a gift from groom to bride,
You'll vow a new vow unto me.
And take me at Your side.

My Groom, come quickly.
Will You draw near?
And pledge love for eternity
Please don't delay.
For my hope grows drear.

My soul longs to connect with Thee.
Dress yourself in light dear Groom,
Then come whisk me away.
Catch me up to be with You
I watch for You and pray.

Hush

Not a whisper, no sound is heard
As His glory fills the room.
The majestic rush of angels' wings
Swept noise as a mighty broom.

Away the clamorous sound removed
Hush fell upon the deep.
A smoky haze did spill in too.
The clouds surround His feet.

I stood in awe of regal presence.
As He lit the room aglow
Then I fell upon my lowly face
For His Holiness did unfold.

No one would faint to gasp a breath
For He too was in the air
And I was humbled by His inclusion
To gain me entrance there.

No sound in ear
I saw with my eye
And heart did feel the rush
To know glory had entered in
Preceded by a hush.

Dark Room

I walk into a large, dark room
No light has filtered in.
Corners laden deep with garbage
To clean where do I begin?

Cobwebs strewn from bottom to top
Time passed since entry gained.
Only shadows venture here,
As the clock does wax and wane.

All hope was soon replaced by fear
Remembering I was alone.
Then rustling whispers heard throughout
Thoroughly chill my bones.

I cowered in fear and trembled deep,
As I quickly came to know.
The voices also troubled my sleep.
Great misery they often bestow.

Then warmth rushed to engulf

Never has it been before.
Now flooding peace was holding me
And light entered the door.

That dark, cold room was once my heart,
        But that one was of old.
For Christ came in and swept it clean
           The glorious light to now behold.

No shoes

I slip my shoes off at the door for the
ground I worship on is holy.
I shiver as I enter in because I am not
There lonely.

His sweet and mighty Spirit has
Preceded me through the door.
It was not long for I found myself
Face down upon the floor.

Hazy the room now appears.
Yes, His glory filled the space.
Mingled with His loving-kindness
Peppered with His grace.

Such an encounter to explain
One simply cannot do.
Unless you enter into covenant
It is secret unto you.

Eagerly I run to the door

My heart is pounding fast.
I know You wait for me on the other
side.

I have but one more task.
Remove the shoes upon my feet.
For the ground I worship on is holy.
Remove your shoes, come now let's go.
He is not there for me only.

No mere existence

Created for glory.
Yours and not mine.
A purpose in the story.
Yours and not mine.

Sending up praises
Yours and not mine.
Basking in graces
Yours and not mine.

Calling on a mighty name
Yours and not mine.
Trusting thc immortal fame
Yours and not mine.

Resting in Your presence
Yours and not mine.
I exist because
I am Yours and not mine.

House of God

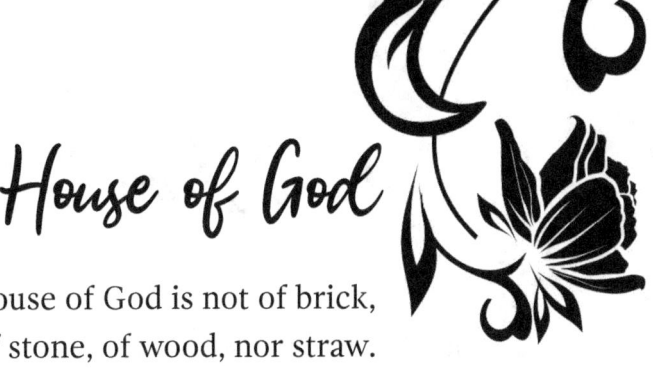

The house of God is not of brick,
Of stone, of wood, nor straw.
The house of God has life within
Not governed by the law.

The place Your Spirit longs to dwell
Is not inside man-made walls.
Your voice indeed is deeply felt.
So my heart shall heed its calls.

I will be the house of God.
My soul shall be Your space.
And now it is there I commune with You,
Until I glance upon Your face.

To be made the house of You is not an easy thing.
One must sweep out the dusty toil,
The worldly life did bring.

A house of God I came to be.
My true calling is fulfilled.
To open up my heart to You
This house must fully yield.

Kingdom warrior

Yes, yes, I do that and all things
Through Christ who strengthens me.
His mighty power shores me up.
Lifted high upon His wings
Within His grace, His mercy's stead.

I find my will to fight.
Within His everlasting Word
I find my daily might.

Conquer to the enemy.
Bring pain to darkness great.
Place your foot on satan's neck.
Burden him with his own weight.

Stand grand soldier gird about
The message that we bring.
Go forth and conquer. Stand ye straight.
Now watch the angels sing.

Of all the glory, massive territory

Laid at the feet of the Holy King.

Out of the ashes

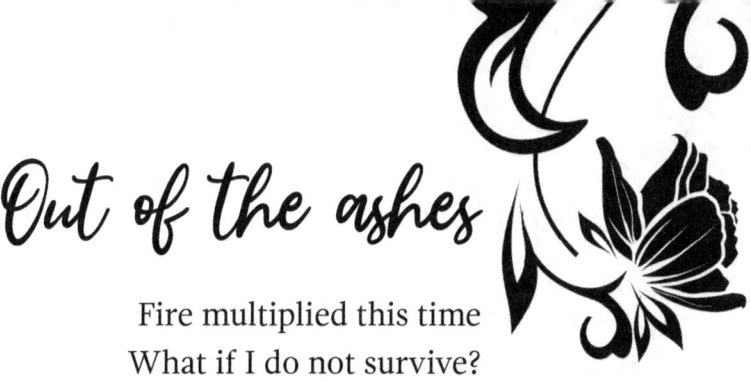

Fire multiplied this time
What if I do not survive?
The minions and the hoards about
They strive to take my life.

Turn up the heat my enemies say.
Make him denounce his King.
For if his God is truly real,
Then deliverance He will bring.

Fire trials began to build and then to lick my bones.
For I was their next helpless meal
Oh I began to groan.

Then like a flood you did rush in,
And rescue became real.
Out of the ashes I arose.
My fate they could not seal.

You hold my spirit in your hands.
I knew that from the start.
You watched my turn to destroy.
But you strengthened my heart.

One drop

It would have taken just one drop
To cleanse me from my sins.
Not because I was so good
But for the power found in Him.

So many ways, Lamb's blood poured out
And spilled upon the earth.
It found its way into my life
Creating in me worth.

He gave His all for all of us
To make us free indeed.
Yes my sister, friend, and neighbor
For you too this man did bleed.

He endured to remove strife
Savior did suffer long.
Stripped away and ripped from life
To remove all my wrong.

One drop of blood was as a flood
That swept the nations clean.
From the past and future too
This sacrifice redeemed.

Peace like a river

Peace like a river
They tell me I need.
Yet the rush of the river
Is but a fresh heart bleed.

The struggles before me
They bow my head.
The sorrows behind me
Have left me for dead.

I trudge along
With heavy so deep.
Prayer buried inside me
My soul, will you keep?

I peeled back the pages
Of your fortified Word
I read in your book
"Be like the bird"

Mount up and fly high.
Your burdens I bear.
Have peace like a river,
For you are always in My care.

O Captain

I yield to thee both ship and sea
O Captain of my destiny.
You who speak to wave and storm.
Calming before it brings me harm.

O Captain Your power I can attest.
For you know Your creation far the best.
And so I yield both ship and sea
To the captain of my destiny.

The ship (my body) You did create.
Formed into this wondrous state.
The sea but is the life You give.
The path You drew, the way to live.

You know me, both within and without.
I am secure, there is no doubt.
And now I yield both ship and sea
To the captain of my destiny.

At the helm You stand a guard.

You face the storms, hail on forward.
As I gain rest, You keep vigil by night.
The waves conquered by Your might.

You show me through Your wage of war.
So many victories You have in store.

At break I see the sun-filled day.
A lighted path to mark the way.
And so I yield both ship and sea
To the Captain of my destiny.

Potter's wheel

Into skillful hands and taken up
Me, without form and void.
Placed upon the Potter's wheel
The Master overjoyed.

Cause this dark and menaced clay
To produce within, a blessed array.
Of His attributes and glory.
His plan to take away my plan.

He works now with such fury.
This crafted wheel circles round and round.
I feel the need to stop.
But the Master of the wheel
Shall mold from base to top.

And so I stay work within His hands
'Til finished He does say.
No longer without form and void
But shapened, useful clay.

Prayer

I lay upon my face and weep
No sorrow but for hope.
My cries to You Your ear incline
My mind a slippery slope.

Forgetting all my Lord has done
You fought my causes well.
The victories are laid at Your feet
For You shall never fail.

My prayers I think they touch the sky.
Because You step in before I die.
And when I lay me down to sleep.
You prove over again, my soul You keep.

With tears of joy and peace renewed.
In prayer I am reminded
Of all that You would do.

On my behalf
Just have the faith.
You see me through
You give me grace.

Proclamation

Shout to God, You are my King.
Gather the four winds to sing.
Let the earth, the mountains quake.
With voice as loud as ocean break.

Our God is God, let us all cry.
May evil tremble gone awry.
Shout to God, You are my King.
Gather the four winds to sing.

Stand erect and now proclaim
The glory of our Savior's name.
Jesus You are Lord of all.
The trees yet bow however tall.

The rocks whisper without shame
He is King, He is King, forever reign.
Shout to God You are my King.
Gather the four winds to sing.

Promise keeper

You assured me in the secret place,
You'd never let me down.
If I should endure until the end,
I would receive a crown.

But You've made good on promises,
This side of eternity.
To keep me safe and in Your care
With me You'll always be.

Though the way so often rough,
And I stumble because of me.
You however, have been rooted,
As deeply as a tree.

So Promise Keeper is Your name,
And now, I shall no more forget
That every promise You have made,
You have so aptly kept.

Proposal

You did not get down on bended knee
Nor flash a glossy ring.
You did not shine it in the sky
Or fancy a song to sing.

But oh You wooed me won my heart.
Just simply who You are.
I can't resist when You've taken part.
To be my Shining Star.

With outstretched hands You rescued me
And said, "Now come away."
Beckoned me deep within my soul
In Your presence I will stay.

You call to me from far and wide.
Come hither and be mine.
I answered and belong to You
I will be Your bride.

Questions and answers

Questions:
Why me Lord?
Why am I sick?
Why am I burdened?
Why am I broken?
Why am I afraid?
Why am I lonely?
Why am I troubled?

Answers.....
Why not you?
My Word says: "Prosper and be in good health, even as your soul does prosper."
My Word says: "I will not allow more on you than you are able to bear."
My Word says: "A broken and contrite heart, I will not turn away."
My Word says: "I have not given you a spirit of fear."
My Word says: "I will stick closer than a brother".
My Word says: "There is no sorrow that can compare to My glory."

Final Answer: Stand on My Word.

Psalm 107:2

I was that girl, she was that girl, he was that guy, and him, him, her, her and you yes you... and yes I said was... why was and not is? Because you... is no more... your you is a was because you are a new you...How? Why? When? Did this occur? Yesterday and the day before is the when. Because He loves you and heard your cry is the why... Because God is and God can so He did is the how.

When your mind tries to force you back to that uncomfortable comfort zone where the whispering voices of "what happened to me when", how "I barely survived yet fccl like the walking dead," schizophrenic faith teetering between what He already proved and what is yet to manifest, what ifs, this is too hard, and life just sucks. Let the redeemed of the Lord SAY SO... SO it's hard...I still have fight left. SO I lost a battle, there is yet a war to be won. SO the day is long, embrace the hour.

SO your health is tried, walk and breathe anyway.

SO you may feel lonely but you are never alone. SO you got life to live and work to do. SO SAY SO.

Rapture

Ready to go up.
Preparing to fly.
On my way to eternity.
Gonna touch the sky.

My Savior is coming back for me.
He'll whisk me away home.
Setting my feet in glory,
Never more to roam.

I feel weightless with just the thought
Of touching eternal sky
Lavishing in perpetual joy
Never more to die.

Infinite light from Heaven's throne
Will illuminate the path.
Forever to endure God's love
Removing all His wrath.

Jesus come, rapture me
Take Your daughter home.
So I may gaze upon Your face
Sitting near Your throne.

Rebuke

We say we love You, but only from our lips.
Our worship is a false fashion show of tips, flips, and trips.

When will our heart break for what breaks Your heart?
When will we stop standing idly by while
The world tears the church apart?

We look so much like sin.
That those who seek You don't know where to begin.

We should be ashamed that we lumber with the herd.
When the Almighty God made us to soar like the Bird.

Awaken my lovely for the time is nigh and only the true heart will be called up high.

Sonlight

Sonlight broke the cloudy morn
And dried the drenching dew.
The clamor deep inside my head
Silenced because of You.

The darkness of my dormant nights
Now cower because of dawn.
On the mountaintops of all my struggles
Now shine the light of the glorious one.

No more shall evening end my day
No matter the turn or tide.
Because you who broke the chains of strife
Have claimed me as Your bride.

With my face turned toward the sky
Your light now burns in me.
Shining out forevermore
Sonlight will always be.

The storm

The thunder shook me to my core
Lightning caused me to hide.
Out of sight on trouble's path
It searched after me far and wide.

The rain hammered down on me
I can no more contain.
The bruises and the scars received
The misery and pain.

You said, "You'd never allow for me
More struggle than I could bear."
I terror dear Lord at the storm around
For I cannot feel You there.

Keep me safe throughout this plight
I plead with each new breath.
Yet I am trusting in Your Word,
Which reads neither height nor depth.

So Lord not even this terrific storm

Which seeks to consume me whole.
Could dare contain nor dare curtail
to keep me from my goal.

3 a.m.

I cannot sleep I have been stirred
Squinting to see the clock.

It's three a.m. try to ignore
But on my heart's door You have knocked.

Throw back the blanket feet on the floor.
Stand up moving out the door.

Head toward the secret place for You desire to
speak to me.
Pleased to sacrifice my sleep
With You I long to be.

Yet Lord You know I must confess
I'd often like to know.
Why do You like to wait until
Three a.m. to show.

Me all the secrets that You hold.
The ones I long to see.
Nevertheless, overjoyed
For in Your presence I long to be.

Throne song

God, Your Word tells me there is a song
Released from Your throne on high.
Not from angels the heavenly hosts,
But from Your own heart's lullaby.

Your song, You sing it over me
I scarcely can conceive
What Word, or thought, or deed, or verse
You'd whisper over me.

A sweetness in the melody
A lightness in the tone.
A touch of honey scented breath
Descending from the throne.

Sing over me oh Sovereign One
In the gentle winds that blow.
May I be pleasing in Your sight,
And You make my face to glow.

Why existence?

Created with care
Fearfully and wonderfully You dare.

To make this person
The I in me.
Tell, tell, what do you see?

Who am I?
What am I to be?
Why do I breathe?
Why do I think?
Surely existence not
Merely for meat and drink.

To have a purpose
There must be a plan.
This wondrous construct
Is simply too grand!

When I meet me

I see that girl, in the distance, so far away, I recognize her frame though the image is blurred. I must get to that girl, I am compelled, drawn to her in an almost mystical way.

She looks almost like me, but more beautiful, she sounds like me, but more knowledgeable, walks like me, except a bit straighter, she bombards the throne of God with words on others behalf, she calls down fire from Heaven, she speaks and mountains move, with expressed boldness and conviction sickness is healed and death turns an about face.

She assaults the kingdom of darkness with never ending force and taking no prisoners, she advances the Kingdom of God increasing the binds of the Lamb's Book of Life.

She is fire and brimstone, she is Proverbs 31, she is the Shunnamite woman, she is Ruth, she is Esther and Hadassah, she is Mary, she is Martha, she is Rahab.

She is epic and worthy of her own story. She is because God is in her and soon we will be one.

Words from the broken place

The weight of it all, I don't want to anymore. So I exhale more deeply than I inhaled and try to expel all God's breath that He breathed into me. Give up? I did. Keep up the work — for what? My heart beats to the rhythm of nothing but pain because the dream killer has come and gone leaving nothing but drain.

Quench the Spirit. What spirit? That river of living water dried up so long ago, exposing first the two feet deep mud that would burden down my walk, cementing my feet to this earth extinguishing every passionate attempt to fly free.

The sun beat both me and the earth I stood upon until we were both left as powder. Now this path — dry, barren, desolate, and devoid. I stumble choking on the dust kicked up by my directionless feet.

I thought I might try one more time, but I didn't have the fight. I thought I might try again, but fear was ruler, was king, was kindred. It was the only entity that refused to leave me. It always served up reassurance by surfacing every chance it got.

Well since I am breathing, since I am not dead. I might as well get on with living. This is not my first time in the broken place and may not be my last but this I know...I never stay here so I won't start now.

Thoughts of the blood

I can't conceive of the loss You felt that
it took to gain us.

I can't conceive the broken heart
You endured to extend trust.
What were You thinking when You sent Your own
Son, in an order to obtain those who
May not ever be won?

I pondered the reasons then but I do not question
Now because I was redeemed, not only me
But others in the crowd. What if I was the only one?
Would You have dared hand over Your only
Begotten Son?

Your Kingdom fractured to make it whole,
redeeming creation was Your only goal.
With my heart turned toward Your will.
My life given over is a thank You real.

Winter no more

In the winter of my confusion
Your voice is hushed from me.
My thoughts slovenly turn to fear.
Surmising alone I would now be.

How quickly I forget the wonders of Your hand.
When to see all of Your power work,
Faith was all You would demand.

The days grow dark and long and chill
As I wrap them with my mind's lies.
He has forsaken you, too far you fall
And my soul felt this deep demise.

But, oh my Savior, you saw fit
To not leave me burdened in despair.
Below You reached to raise me up
With graciousness and care.

I felt inward me begin to warm
Under the authority of Your touch.

As the winter in my heart and soul
Lost dominion through this river's rush.

Your Spirit moved upon
The face of my deep,
And carried the frost away.

Now I reside in a warming sweep.
On the crest of a sunny spring day.

Worried

Let's face it the mind unchecked can become a cornucopia of bad memories, vain imaginations, unspoken prayer, what ifs, negative words from "well-meaning friends," fears not manifest, fear that have manifest, and the devil running amok. I have to admit with much discomfiture and transparency, that I am a worrier. As a child I continually created and completed scenarios that ended in the "worst case." As a young mother the sight of blood would quickly push me into thoughts of appendage dismemberment or worse.

The tragic death of my younger brother on the cusp of our early thirties launched me into a whole new plain of mental and emotional anguish. I believed for years that death was all around, circling me and those I held dear. If my children had a bug bite, go to the hospital. It could be brown recluse. If they had a sore throat, go to the hospital. Streptococcus can go to the brain, and fevers were potentially meningitis. (Now I believed I had a very strong argument for the

meningitis fear after losing a three-year-old cousin to that illness.) When my children would fall and hit their heads, I would not sleep the first two days and then set a clock to wake them up every three hours until "they were no longer at risk for

brain bleeding." Flash forward to the sudden death of my father five years ago and I must admit that each time my mother does not answer her phone when I call that I am left a heart palpating, hand sweating, word jumbled, somebody go knock on my mother's door mess, a fearful mess, a worry filled mess.

Sometimes plagued with fear of harm by "friends not friends," roofied drinks, drug addiction, date rape, police involvement, and yes even murder and suicide.. You know, just the garden variety daily struggles of life (enter sarcasm).

Maybe your fears aren't as insane as mine, maybe you are reading all of this and saying "Jeez, she's got it bad." Maybe you are reading this portion of the book and feel as if you are facing a mirror and this chapter is a finger pointing directly at you. Let me be the first to say that it is easier to tell someone don't worry than it is to stop worrying. I have had guilt because I have been told that if I worry I don't trust God. I have been told that if you have an ounce of fear then you have zero faith. I have been told that you cannot truly be a Christian and have fears. Before you quote another scripture to me, I know God's word says that HE has not given us the spirit of fear.

I know that it is followed by HIM giving us power, love, and a sound mind. What I want someone to tell me is how to truly rid yourself of fear, how do you truly "lay it down?" I will not pretend that I know the answer but I do want to encourage you by telling you that you are not alone in your plight.

I also know beyond a shadow of a doubt that you can not only outlive but also overcome the situations that cause worry and fear. I often refer to a singular thought process when things become almost overwhelming. Well I ain't dead; so I guess I will fight on.

The funny thing is that this thought process works for me. Now it may not work for you but I believe

that breath in my body insures one more day toward Victory, one more day

toward strength, one more day toward one more day. Therefore, I can do all things through Christ who strengthens me.

We all have days when even our best game face won't diminish our look of someone on the precipice, someone on their last leg but if you have a "last leg" I dare you to stand on it and see the salvation of the Lord.

What if?

What happens when words come with no idea of what to say?
Do you simply let the moment pass with discordant Dismay?

What happens when the heart is full but the soul, Not so much?
Do you join the rabble anyway, content with a Lackluster touch?

The questions outnumber by far that which we agree Is unequivocally true.
Do you bother to ponder the question or let the Question ponder you?

What happens, truly happens if one day we all Awake?
To answers rushing in like a tsunami produced by a Knowledge quake?

When I have finished my story and HE has finished The chapter of me.
    Will I be wiser than before or just

merely hope to be?
The "facts" have never concerned me

Because they Are seen through glasses rose.
"Wisdom" often painted innuendo decorated
Verbose.

Patterns and sequences awaken me to pen them to
The page.
Remembering to dictate every word whether of joy,
Fear, or rage.

Bleeding sleep as I ramble about the yes, the no, the
Why.
Sleep then fornicates with me as I dream the can,
The know, don't try.

Other life forces proceeding me left an indication
None.
Never a true representation of what really must be
Done.

Stumbling through the dark wondering if all a
Dream or grotesquely true.

I am ashamed to also admit I've wondered if
Goosebumps are even from You.

I cannot stomach no more emotional
Output as the fakery has me drained.
The claim to know but be far from You is truth that
Most should proclaim.

Church as usual, no healing, none set free. A show
Drenched in human pride.

Shouts, tongues, dance steps to the left, steps to the
Right, throw your head back, arms
Wrenched, face contorted as we fight.

Yes, mimic what we've been taught is holy.
Flesh deemed what makes you proud.
These fascist ideologies we dare not rebut aloud.

With that said, I am still at a loss to believe all I've
Been told is true.
Never questioning possibility but assured there is so
Much more to YOU.

To emulate the words of the Book we
Much needs Start over again.

For our actions have been to glorify self
and Camouflage our sin.

What if all was laid bare; our feet, our hearts, the
Room?
Would we venture to do it right this time or return
To whited sepulchers and tombs?

Lord, the words I speak interpret that I long to
Know Your name.
Far greater than the outside appearance and what
My mouth shall only proclaim.

I ask dear Lord that my different drum beats loud
To a decibel high enough drowning out those in the
Crowd.

It sometimes aches that I am so different, separated
From the rest.
Sheepishly preaching to the choir when tis? You
Who knows me best.

No longer a caged bird waiting to sing, I yearn to be
Made free.
Pondering never more the secrets of eternity that I
Secretly do not see.

Threshing floor

I must admit, I do not like
The process to become

Something of use to my Savior Lord.
A product of the Son.

You placed me on the threshing floor.
And began to beat my bones
Necessary You became violent
For my heart had turned to stone.

I did not conceive within my mind
When I spoke the prayer.
Use me Lord, whatever Your will
Lest I would but dare

To count the cost oh think it through.
Considering all I must do.
To be the one that You would use.
To carry out Your plan for me
I would feel the bruise.

The threshing floor is where I am made
Over and again.
Yielding up my everything

The other shoe

The sermon was over and women began to flood the altar. My job (that I took upon myself) was to care for those who came for prayer and were lucky enough to receive a touch from God. Tissues...check, prayer covers...check, oil anointed hands...check. Let's do this. Catch, lay, cover, repeat.

Suddenly, I realized that everyone around me was on the floor, my feet seemed stuck like cement, and the eye contact that I tried so hard to avoid was now inevitable. My mind said, "Look strong and confident...NOW! NOW! NOW!" I can't because the truth is — my heart is broken, and my soul is starved for attention from the Lord.

She approaches me. This woman I have known for 21 years has had the uncanny ability to come out of shadows at some of my most spiritually abase times, and speak a word to my soul. A word that has the power to unleash the "it's time to fight" in me. She touches the place where God desires to breathe and

blow upon my very soul, pushing death away for another season. She would be considered a "nobody" to some.

(Although, she probably prefers it that way.) She is not a Bishop, Apostle, or even a Pastor. She does not hold a public office, and is not often witnessed as a public speaker.

However, she is a retired school administrative assistant (what we used to call a secretary). When I met Mrs. Goode, she was sitting behind a very small desk in a very small front office, with a sliding glass window. She looked as if she was preparing to sign you in to see the doctor, as opposed to the 1000 other things she did on a daily basis: taking temperatures, passing out band aids, and calling parents of sick children. Her voice would have measured almost forgettable if her radiant, pure spirit hadn't already seized you with her sincere "good morning."

My first encounter with her was "I have a problem." I shared it — I was at her mercy and the mercy of her superiors. Instead of the standard spill of "well, this is policy. I am sorry, but those are the rules for everyone" or "you missed the deadline." Her answer instead,

"Well let's just pray about it, and then let's believe God for it! The next thing I know, that woman was all in my business and my personal space. She was grabbing both my hands and stretching them upward while instantaneously calling upon the name of Jesus on my behalf.

I was so caught off guard that the first thing to pop into my mind was, "Wow. Her breath is so minty fresh." I still remember what the problem was. I remember God worked it out. He would continue to work that problem out each time it reared its ugly head.

Over twenty years later, I still realize that I would rather have the phone answering, computer tapping, parent calming, child fever taking, newsletter typing, classroom babysitting (so the teacher can potty), praying down the house, and getting heavenly results, private school receptionist in my corner than a prominent Bishop or "bigtime" televangelist ANYDAY!

Anyway, flash forward and back to the altar call.

I haven't had contact with Mrs. Goode in about three years. Nevertheless, there she was all up in my face again. She put

her left hand on my shoulder and pointed at me with her fingers on the other, right in my face.

My six-inch heels caused me to tower over her but she was in no way intimidated. "Peaches, I see you. Now, this might hurt your feelings, but I gotta say what God told me to say. I know that's what you want too."

At once my hands rise above my head as an act of surrender to the Spirit of God I instantly feel flowing from this retired secretary. My body, especially my legs begin to shake like a newborn deer as Holy Spirit washed over me. Suddenly, I feel like a baby bird and Mrs. Goode was the bird bringing the worm to the nest to feed my starving soul. In the spirit, my mouth was wide open. I was ready for what was coming my way.

She begins, "you are always waiting for the other shoe to drop. Yes, devastating things have happened, but you attend every day waiting for the very God that you adore to smite you just one more time.

You cannot even properly attend to the things that give you joy because of your constant entertainment of thoughts like: Who is going to die next? What else can go wrong? The spirit of fear has taken root. The Word of God says, 'He has not given us a spirit of fear.' He has however, 'given us a spirit of power, love, and a sound mind."

She said, "Now I know you got power, the way you carry yourself and so many others around you. I have seen your love in action. The sound mind, it is also a choice. Either you gonna have it, or you ain't. He gave it to you. However, you have allowed the broken places, the hurt, and the devices of the enemy to cloud your thoughts. Your hurts are not uncommon to man. You have supernatural power working in every one of your situations." Then she says it, the one scripture I must admit that I had come to despise. (I know what you are thinking…"This is blasphemy. You are not allowed to hate scripture.") You do not understand. Every self-appointed spiritual counselor, pew pastor, or nosy friend has quoted this scripture to me continually over the course of three years of what I now so affectionately call "The Dark Ages."

When I meet the Apostle Paul, he may even get a karate chop for penning that verse. Who else can be that famous for surviving shipwrecks, snake bites, imprisonment, but still be able to tell us to "get over ourselves."

You are still wondering what the verse is that incites me to violence in my private thoughts. (The one that basically tells us not to whine because God is taking all the bad and good situations and reworking them together to create a positive outcome, a complete beautiful finished product) I had just days earlier confided in my hubby that I planned to "throat punch" the next person who quoted Romans 8:28 to me. Yeah, that's the one. Only, I didn't punch Mrs. Goode, I melted on her. A heavy heart, meshed with a smile, tears met a runny nose, and my arms dropped and draped the shoulders of this older woman. She bore the weight of my body and my broken spirit. She whispered that God desired to uproot the root of bitterness that I was carrying and trying so hard to suppress. God was going to release me from that and the fear. I only needed to yield. So I did.

God is so faithful and attentive to His children. Mrs. Goode has moved back into the shadows again until God allows her to "see me."

The cost

The change in your pocket is yours to keep.
The price already paid caused many to weep.
The knock upon the door of your heart
Caused you to be one of many set apart.

Since your blood was not royalty it could not pay the cost.
Your soul is worth more than the contents of an alabaster box.

The provision made was uncountable, worth more than rubies rare,
Yet, even the richest men of old could never pay the fare.

The ability to render recompense due
Was fathomless to both me and you.
Imagine your blood, spilled on the ground.
And that thing which you created for beauty now
Fashioned into a painful crown.

Imagine your child sacrificed on an altar
To atone for all flesh, the one birthed
From you... now you witness his death.

Can you say you would offer to take the
place of another?
Especially those who would never receive

you as the lover — of their soul.

The cost was so great that only one had the worth,
The unequaled ability to move Heaven and save
Earth.
Oh, let the inhabitants count the cost,
Of a blood washed soul no longer lost.

Our part is to accept what was to Him not free,
And in doing so, we shall be made free, and made
Free yes free indeed.

What was the cost? The greatest story ever told,
God walked among us as man, a wonder to behold.
Freely receive what has cost everything to be given,
Now your way was literally bought for you to enter
Heaven.

The blood sacrifice more precious than gold and the
Son of Man; Majestic;
A wonder to behold.

My own rivers

I have known rivers for they run deeply through my soul.
I have known rivers, they are the ebb and tide of what my mind and heart yet holds.

I often fear the river because the art of swimming was never taught to me. I guess it's one of the many lessons for which the art... conveniently forgot...ten million years it feels since I needed not be afraid.
Ten million years it feels that I writhed in this watery grave.

The rivers' tumultuous flow changes speed
And direction only to allow me time to surface for air, only time to gasp one more breath.

No not enough breath to say I will make it to the other side
Just enough breath to give me confidence that I will see my own demise.
I have known rivers, the failures of this life,

I have known rivers, between the colors so much strife.
I have known rivers, in my mother's eye

never good enough, I have known rivers
at the not so innocent hands of A father's
touch,

I have known rivers, pretending that proximity
equals love,
I have known rivers, when doing all that could be
Done would still never be enough.

I have known rivers, I have known rivers I have
known rivers
I will however, traverse the waters just as I have
Done before.
I will continue to gasp for that breathe until I can
Gasp no more.

I have only died a thousand deaths and if necessary
I am prepared to die a thousand more.
And will continue to know the rivers until I pass
Through eternities doors.

Humans are like a breath of air and their lifespan is
A fleeting shadow

Psalm 144:4 GWT

In the shadow of death

Death Realized

Why does life become schizophrenic in the face of death? Why do we say that someone died of natural causes when they die at an old age? If death is humanity's reward for sin, then why aren't cancer, AIDS, heart failure, asthma, tumors, cystic fibrosis, diabetes, multiple sclerosis natural causes?

We state that death is not from God. Why? Because it hurts us? So is childbirth. Yet, we call it a gift. If we are His creation, then He does with us at His will. We claim He is all-knowing, all-powerful, and never does wrong, but we believe that the transition from this life is a terrible act committed against us.

We are quick to dispel the idea that we continue to reap from our iniquity. If that is the case, why do we see a lull in the natural things when we don't tithe and give offerings? Why do positive situations turn negative when we disobey God? Why can't we realize

that when we quote the scripture of Jesus coming to give life and life more abundantly that (1) we have to be living

in order to die so He gave us life and (2) who are we to judge what abundant life (time) is for any man? Do we know whether someone's appointed days were 30 years and they lived for 50 so the abundance was 20. What if someone's days went from 12 years to 25 years? What if 4 years to 15 years? What if your own days were numbered at 35 and abundance were 65... a baby with 0 given 5 years. Would we change our outlook on death then?

A heart stopped on this side of eternity is a blessing as we cannot dwell with Him in our flesh for no man shall see Him that is still wrapped in this human carcass. From the dust we came and from the dust we shall return. In the face of death we forget that God has become reaper of His own harvest and has come to collect the fruit of His planted manifested seed. The filth returns to the ground. That which is hallowed returns to Him who planted it, cultivated it, cropped it, fertilized it, and now has come to harvest it.

What better feeling than seeing the manifestation of your seed right in front of you more beautiful than when it all first began—Bravo God.

I have my follies. I ask God, "Why do you let a 5 year old that worships in song and prayer die after losing a leg to cancer. Why do you let a 30 year old die from a motorcycle wreck 3 miles from home after bringing him from 6 hours away on the same apparatus. Why do tumors grow in the wombs of mother as they nurse their new babies at their breast not knowing they will never see them grow to be adults. Why does life conceive in a womb only to drift away before viability or rather, departs from the womb and take its last breath wrapped in a swaddling blanket and laying in mommy's arms.

Why God, why do you allow this?" He answered me with this, "My children will never know the joyous mysteries of death until they themselves stand in front of me clothed in My spirit so I tell them, they are mine, and they have been quickened."
To take off the worrisome flesh and walk freely in

spirit inhaling and exhaling the very breath of God. The very act of death may come in a form of violence to the flesh as it is literally ripping the spirit away from it. Those of us who belong to God will then be granted the gift of walking in

our true state which is spirit created after the image and likeness of God.

Quickened:— verb (used with object)
1. to make more rapid; accelerate; hasten:
2. to give or restore vigor or activity to; stir up, rouse, or stimulate:
3. to revive; restore life to
— verb (used without object)
1. to become more active, sensitive, etc.
2. to become alive; receive life.
3. (of the mother) to enter that stage of pregnancy in which the fetus gives indications of
life.
4. (of a fetus in the womb) to begin to manifest signs of life

Dear John letter

(A break up)

I went to the doctor last week because I have been sick for quite some time. I have not been able to stand upright. It's strange that when I go to church, my stomach gets uptight; I vomit. I had an itch I could not scratch. I tried every medication I could find: over the counter this, and over the counter that. The remedy was always temporary. On every occasion was left writing, and worse off than I was before the fix.

I could never find an actual remedy, even though I looked in every place familiar to me. My mind whirling, swirling, reeling and jeering. What pray tell, oh what in satan's Hell was wrong with me? I was healthy and glowing just months ago, but recently my health has reached an all-time low. It's true, I have been sick before, but never like this. I believe I was dying. I am sure I was dying. My eyes were yellow, sick with pain. I could not even work to pursue

earthly gain. People told me they could see the sickness. My flesh, gray — tinged with the hue of dirt. The way I walked,

and even my talk suggested I was in the murk. When I came to myself, I realized

that all I had tried to rid myself of this illness was in fact contributing to it. The sickness was becoming more profound by the day.

You see, the beginning symptoms were mild in nature and often random. A variant hiccup, some blurred vision, and the most annoying itch. Soooo after holding my breath until nearly losing consciousness, rubbing my eyes and glaring dazed and confused, or after fighting not to scratch and becoming reconciled to the fact that the itch would only be abated by twisting and contorting into the most egregious postures...

Gradually my hiccups got worse. There were random popups out of nowhere. The choice to choose wrong, so I did. Also, because they managed to go as quickly as they appeared, I did not think they would have a lasting affect. It soon became hard to breathe.

The blurred vision. Let's just say I was literally stumbling in the dark. It was if I had blinders on and someone had turned out the lights.

The itch was definitely the worst of all the symptoms. It mocked me the more I itched the more I scratched. The more I scratched, the more I itched. Consumed from head to toe — no part left unscathed. I went to the doctor. Not just any doctor, but a specialist.

During my consultation I was given two diagnoses. I was shocked by neither; especially after I realized that my actions were the catalyst of my illness and consequently my demise. Oh, I bet you want to know what the doctor said was wrong with me. Well, I had an STD. Nooo. It is not what you think. I had a Sinfully Transmitted Disease.

I was also pregnant, and I didn't qualify for the morning after pill because I was already too far along. The Doctor assured me that He had the cure for what all was ailing me. I would need surgery. He stated I would be quite uncomfortable, but it was necessary to save my life.

I was placed on the operating table and he began to pull, stretch, and cut all without anesthesia stating I needed

to be awake and experience the monster inside me, in hopes that I would not fall into this predicament again. It was more

ugly and more disgusting than I had anticipated. It looked just like me and nothing like me all at the same time, and the smell — there are no words to describe how foul is the stench of rotten flesh.

That baby was not a real baby. I was pregnant with sin. I was pregnant with my own lusts, and the seeds of wickedness deposited by you had been released into the womb of my soul and implanted, multiplied and was alive inside me all the while producing death within me. Nooo, that fetus was not human but it was humanistic fulfilling its fleshly purpose. It was a parasite to my eternal soul.

After the procedure, I was moved to a different room and asked to uncover everything. The doctor proceeded to apply a red ointment on me from head to toe. The Doctor instructed me to apply the ointment daily and allow it to absorb. He cautioned me that it was necessary to guard against the Sinfully Transmitted Disease.

He also remarked that it was mandatory that I break up with you immediately. If I did not, the illness would return full force and I would surely die. Sooo, consider this our break up...a dear John letter... because without you, my life is much, much better. And yes, the Doctor cured me. Oh how He adores me. By the way, I am pregnant again, and it ain't yours.

Conversation with a counterfeit

I am sorry. I am butting in, but I thought I heard you say you were a Christian? No, I am pretty sure you said you were a Christian. Ohhh, you are; well let me enlighten you. I hate to tell you it's a shame you're lame and got no game but most of all you got no flame. You're dark inside no spark inside just dust inside where the rust abides It's a shame you fool yourself, you've amassed a wealth that doesn't pay the bill or make you want to diss your will or live a life of truth or dress your soul in blood covered proof so, you're a Christian.

All that is seen is a life of continued sin and the willful spiritual death of men walked out through earthly ties, flesh wrapped lies and all who partake of this buffet dies Believe your own lies, see life in your own eyes making Hell your home through what you think you know Dictionaries define a Christian as someone who exemplifies in their own life the teachings of Christ or those who exhibit a spirit proper to a follower of Jesus Christ, oh that's you? If it is you and you be a true seeker, then come on up here and you be the speaker.

Tell us how you live a Christ-filled life when you can't manage to empty your days of naughtiness and strife. Pray tell how you face the day when you don't even call His name out. Unless you need a favor, a trick, a bobble, or a disclaimer to get you from under the hammer.

The pain, the grief when you don't have, you fail to release into the atmosphere the only name to be feared. Well, "she's judging," you say, but I cannot apologize for my way, because I can't labor in your vineyard of forbidden fruit, because I cannot locate fallow ground around a rotten root. You quote scripture to me, "Judge not lest you be judged," and I remind you twist not the scripture lest you be like satan. Judgment begins at the house of God if you were living right then you wouldn't be hatin' on those who live the life you fake, on those who walk the path you failed to take.

So taket hat my "Christian" friend as you consume dark life your entertainment filled with murder, homosexuality, zombies, witchcraft, fornication, foul

language and strife. So you call yourself a "Christian," sadly we can't tell you apart maybe it is the company you

keep, or the conversation of your heart. Whatever it is keep lying to yourself so you don't have to die to yourself.

Just continue to blame it on people like me, people with fresh fruit on the tree. If you're going to do it then do it right, come out of the darkness and into the light. Quit the "fake it till you make it." No more sorry excuse. Stop feeding yourself lies committing spiritual abuse, if you're going to claim Him then be like Him in each and every way not foolishness one through six and then a "holy roller" on Sunday.

So you call yourself a "Christian" but your name He's gonna spew because time is coming to an end and God's longsuffering is almost through. Don't worry about the sinners I will preach to them later I'm talking to you Christian faker.

STOP IT!

Wedding day

My wedding dress is in the making
Each moment I must prepare.
To meet upon that hallowed day
Spotless with much care.

My garment shall be purely white.
The clouds will all turn blue.
When the very last spark of light is sewn on,
To the hem of my garment new.

He shall frame my face with glory.
My lamp will be well filled.
A new chapter in my story.
The covenant duly sealed.

When we amass for the wedding feast,
A celebration it shall be
Forevermore we shall be joined
The Bridegroom, His Father, and me.

God is a murderer

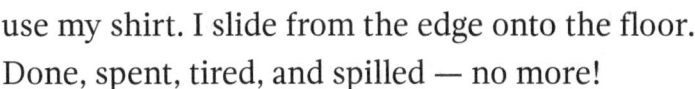

I sit on the couch, wet face, sleeve drenched, no tissues necessary; just use my shirt. I slide from the edge onto the floor. Done, spent, tired, and spilled — no more!

Why so much in such a short time? My mind offers no consolation, no help, no reason nor rhyme. My limit is met or was so, three dramatic episodes not four tragedies ago. With back in a slump, arms limp on the floor, hands upturned in a painful wrench, looking through swollen and blurred eyes is a chore.

I don't need a show. I don't need a circus. I don't need Job's friends. I am contently discontent to sit in my own space, my mind and my soul feeling sorry for themselves. No one to aid my mending and nothing left but to belt out one more verse before I take to death.

"God you are trying to kill me!!! Why?! Have I not served you well?! Ohhh, I believe You had to know these trials would murder me yet into my life they all did flow!"

Realizing I was accusing God, I became afraid (knowing that Hell fire is real. I slid a pillow from the couch and allowed myself to curl around it in a defeated fetalistic (if that is a real word) manner.

Changing my tone and delivery, I again addressed the issues of life which felt like violence, even attempted murder as best as I could label it.

"God," I said weakly, "did you try to kill me? "Are you trying to make me die?" A deep resounding yet inexplicably quiet voice (His voice) spoke to me. His answer; a shock, a jolt, the electric chair to all my foolish human knowledge and so called gained wisdom and insight as to who God is.

"My daughter." He called me ever so gently as if attempting to prepare me for what He as the all-knowing knew I would not be prepared. "My daughter, I tried to kill you. I will kill you and kill everything that is you, everything that is flesh, and everything that is darkness. To be like you is not to be like Me so yes, I tried to murder you."

"What"! I interjected. Confused and quite upset, yet a bit amused by the answer that was the polar opposite of

what I expected. "My goodness Lord." I exclaimed within not uttering a word without. "No." He echoed. "My goodness

and that is exactly why I did what I did." "My daughter, if I allow you to stay in this realm of self-pleasing, self-admonishing, self-indulgent, self centered, self-entitlement, self-sanctification, and this realm of self-existence, then what kind of God, what kind of Master, what kind of Father would I be?"

Feeling a little salty since the conversation was a tad less formal than previous ones between the Murderer and myself, I spoke with satiric humor, attempting to give an answer to combat His statement with my contemplation of His work done on me. "Well, I guess You would be a Father that spoils His kids and tries to make them happy no matter what."

"I could do that." He replied, not placating to my irreverent tone. "Until the end, when all of you is fulfilled, your days on Earth complete, and I withdraw my breath from your fleshly frame and you stand before me in your true form — soul and heart uncovered. You who without my intervention would be deemed vile, destitute, filthy, corrupt, unworthy, stinking, and simply not mine. Would I then be appraised as unjust or inequitable?"

"Because I know what needs to come out so that I may come in, I do what is necessary to remove every weight of sin. Now you, My daughter, did often times remark that GIVE YOURSELF AWAY and you My precious fanciful one. Show me your face you'd often say. So, I did gaze upon your heart for who could know it save none but me. You meant the words you sang and said them with conviction and purity. Now you my sweet, were made of stone so chisel was not enough to break. Ohh yes. I have to murder you in order to retrieve the diamond in the rough."

"Even though you lay in torment, you are where I'd have you be. To finish putting you to death would be pleasurable to me. For when your death is full and complete, you will rise and live true life, no longer self-indulgent, pious, and full of strife."

"No more pity for yourself! Stand up and wipe your face! Do not be shamed before your trials nor hang your head

in such disgrace. Tell that foolishness, that is flesh, to under subjection be and let the words I speak to you keep you in

perfect peace. These afflictions are hard to bear simply because you cannot have your way. If you shall endure until the end, then lift your hands and say, 'I am crucified with Christ; nevertheless, I live, but not I but Christ that lives in me so that the life I now live in the flesh I live by faith in the Son of God who loved me and gave Himself for me.'"

So I said it. My once limp hands were now raised toward the Murderer who I now admonished as the Lover of my soul and I reverently whispered with different tears streaming down my face. "God. You tried to murder me. Your desire is to murder me. And so... I DIE.

www.ingramcontent.com/pod-product-compliance
Lightning Source LLC
Chambersburg PA
CBHW072042110526
44592CB00012B/1518